MOSAIC OF POEMS

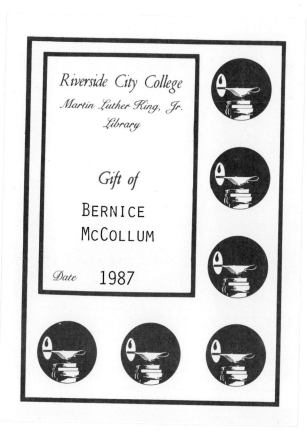

MOSAIC OF POEMS

Here and There, Then and Now

By

Bernice Claire McCollum

Bernice Claire McCollum

THE GOLDEN QUILL PRESS
Publishers
Francestown   New Hampshire

Library of Congress Catalog Card Number 86-81932

ISBN 0-8233-0425-6

Printed in the United States of America

In Fond Memory of
Elsie Emily Smith
Friend and Companion for Forty-Seven Years

With Deep Appreciation of
Lois McCollum Satterburg
My Much-Loved Sister
Who Assisted with the
Technicalities of Preparing the Manuscript

With Affection and Gratitude to
My Students
1927—1956 at
Coachella Valley Union High School
Thermal, California 92274
as well as to
Faculty and Friends
All of Whom Contributed to
My Understanding and Appreciation of Life

ACKNOWLEDGMENTS

Some of the poems in this volume previously appeared in the following publications: *Dialogue with the Blind, Driftwind, Western Poetry,* and *Westward.*

CONTENTS

FOREWORD

Dear Reader,

If you derive even half the pleasure from reading these poems that I have had in writing them, we shall both know something about fulfillment.

From early childhood through teaching and retirement I was an avid reader with interest in biography, economics, geography, language, natural history, psychology, sociology, and travel. My second love, the study of piano, also continued from childhood through retirement.

A crisis came in 1973 when drastically impaired sight made reading of both print and musical notes impossible. "Talking Books" received through the Braille Library Service help to fill the reading void, but I cannot express adequately the great loss of the piano.

If any of these poems have touched your mind or heart, comments would be very much appreciated.

Write to: Bernice C. McCollum
34606 Avenue B
Yucaipa, CA 92399

MOSAIC OF POEMS

ON READING EMERSON'S "THE POET"

Everyone senses the
stuff of poetry.
It is the essence
of the world
about us.

Oh, sunrise and
sunset
bright noon
moonlight balm,
you are poetry.
The myriad
aspects of earth
meadow, wood,
mountain or hill
are all equally
noble for
nature knows not
great nor small.

Only to think of
water,
brook, river,
cascade, sea
is to know
delight.

The daring and
delicacy
of flowers
in infinite
shades
can be
a daily lesson.

Forget not
man's work.
His simplest tools
have nobility
of purpose and
beauty of use.
His toil is seen
in field and factory
in care and
growth of
dumb creatures
not less touched than he
by grace.

Words
unthinkingly used
by all
were at their
inception in
lost antiquity
epochal
and each

itself
poetic.

The poet uses
words
in new sense
and sequence.
Thus they incite
new vision
excite a psychic
rhythm
exalt the spirit.

Our response
is to
the spirit of
wonder
imagination.
We seek
transcendence.

Past ages
had their poets
to inspire their
people.
In our tribulation
may we hear
and heed
the words of our
poet-seers.

WORDS

Words are dear . . . are meant to be;
they can fetter or make you free.
Some are friendly, deep, and round;
others you treasure just for sound.
Like shining jewels in the sun
they are yours to use, once won.

Some are sonorous, bold, and strong;
their majestic rhythms carry you along.
Some whimper, murmur, hush, and subside;
others cling closely and forever abide.
Let these accountants of manifold treasure
pay out tirelessly in endless measure.

A BAD NIGHT

You are weary
really tired.
Bed is so inviting.
You are settled so
comfortably. Now
to sleep.

But you don't.
You lie quietly,
breathe rhythmically,
relax your
muscles. All
of no use.

There is that soothing
sound of a train in
the distance.
Yes, actually, there
is a train. Maybe
a year from now it
will have rolled
away for good.
The train was
for real in earlier
times. Everybody
went to the depot
to see the "flyer"
whoosh through

the town by day. At
night you listened for
the virile
thumping
as the flying sparks
briefly lighted
the black night.
The old coal burner
had it all over today's
sleek
diesel job.

There is a dog
barking
all too near.
It is a particularly
annoying, yappy
sound. And you
like dogs, too.
Now he is quiet,
thank heaven.
The answering
is far enough
away to blend
pleasantly.

It is really too bad
to be near
a freeway
especially when

there is a
rise and
trucks change
gear.

By George, there is
the bark of coyotes
or more likely just one
that can sound like
a pack.
There is still a
little patch of desert.
Soon the poor beasts
won't be able to
sustain life
the way man
devours space.

There is the siren.
Some unlucky devil has
fallen asleep at the
wheel to end up
at the hospital, or
morgue. Or, perhaps
some fool just
had to hurry to
save two minutes at
his destination.
Now he'll never
reach it.

You stealthily slide
out of bed with shaded
flashlight to
sneak to the kitchen
for something hot
to drink.
The hot water bottle
may relax you,
too.
Down the hall
your brother snores
quietly.
Lucky bastard!

Now you are back
in bed.
Stentorian yawns
presage sleep—
surely.

Damn it!
There is a cock
crowing. He
must be crazy.
Your luminous dial
shows it is
only one-thirty.

You'll feel like
the devil
in the morning.

There is that
important conference
at ten; and
old Walker is
a stinker. You'll
need all your wits.
You'll feel like
cheery good mornings
all around! Yah . . .

That plane is
making a lot of
noise. It must
be flying pretty low.

What will it be like
in ten more years
more planes
more cars
more noise
more pollution
more people.

Maybe no one
will sleep then.

This will never do.
You must get to sleep.
You wonder what
time it is.

Just as you thought—
nearly sunrise.
You can't possibly get
more than three hours'
sleep.

You do feel
drowsy at last.

You suddenly
drop into a
velvet black
hole of sleep.

Blast it! There
is the alarm!

June 1971

A MUTUAL GIFT

Tell me
that you love me
that my exultant
heart
may sing.

Kiss me, love,
for my mouth
hungers for
the sealing
of your lips.

Hold me close.
Thus only
do I know
peace—
deep peace.

Our love
inscrutable
a mutual gift
endures.

May 1946

A NEW LIFE

No age is too great
to begin anew.

Real trouble can
bow the shoulders
dull the eye
make mournful
the voice
slow the step and
hurt the heart.

That is true
but with courage
the path ahead
shows
places to rest
and refresh the
spirit. For you
are making a
new start
knowing that
you did your
best.

You had to learn
through suffering
that no one can bear
another's
burden.

Each must find his way
with compassion
for others and
awareness of
his own
need.

Once again
will come
serenity and
peace. There will be
joy in the
brightness of
day, the
shelter of
night.

You will feel
the warm
support of
those who
love you.

Life will
again be
good.

May 1971

A NIGHT ON TABLE-TOP MOUNTAIN

After three hours' walk and climb
my pack is slipped off.
Muscles relax
gratefully.
It is a *good* tired feeling.
The noise, dirt, and murk
of the city are
left behind;
the mind's whirring
machinery
slows down.

    My back rest is a
    smooth boulder.
    Before me, out and
    down,
    Table-Top Mountain
    slopes away.

        I must have dozed
        for shadows are longer.

        A few forays provide
        wood for a fire.
        That burning,
        I start simple preparations
        for supper.

Somehow scout squirrels
and jays
are alerted.
Tidbits reward
their bright-eyed
vigilance.
How good supper
tastes!

Camp chores done
I walk toward the
sunset.
This is the hour
I most cherish
for its different display.
Sometimes it is
so beautiful
I know it is well
it is evanescent.

Tonight the western sky
is a pure expanse
of gold.
Great pines are
dark against its
brightness.

The glow dims
and is replaced

by a bluish grey
then darkening
blue.

Mid September air
grows chill.
After a warm-up
near the
embers,
a camper's bed
beckons.
Soon I am snug
and warmth envelops
me.

How pure and pine-scented
the air.
The constant wind
through the trees
increases the
music of their
motion
to create a special
kind of
silence.

The owl's hoots
are heard by all
creatures
within the confines

of his lugubrious
call.

The stars are
undimmed.
I hold my breath
as one, falling,
flashes in a tiny
segment of the
great arching
heaven.

It travels too fast for me
to make a
wish.

A cone thuds.
Drowsily I speculate
on the chances of a
pine
resulting from this
random propagation.
Little creatures will
strip the cone of
fertility
leaving only a
husk to
disintegrate to form
a minute particle
of earth's accreting
mantle.

A long, contented
interval of
peace.
I am almost over the
brink of
consciousness.

It is morning!
The sun last seen
trailing gold
is now bringing up a
pink dawn.

Soon I'll be
descending to my
work-a-day world
renewed and
strengthened
by my night
on Table-Top Mountain.

Pearblossom, California 1971

A PLACE TO REST

Walking in a strange city
I saw beautiful trees
in the distance
and thought
"There is a park."

But I was mistaken.
It was a resting
place
for the dead.

For the dead
who see not
neither do they
hear
nor feel.

With their
last breath
their spirit left
the integument
that had
sheltered it.

Honor should be
done to the body.

Best it be
returned to
elements by
pure flame.

Not in stone
but loving
hearts be
they remembered
until their
children, too,
join the
multitude.

The living have
need
of a place to
rest.
Wearied bodies
and burdened minds can be
renewed.
On green grass
our poor feet
find relief
from pavement.

Our eyes
follow the

boles
of trees to
whispering
canopy wherein
birds sing
their joy.

Trees grow
unhurried.
Birds have no
care for
the future.

Only in quietude
and peace
do we know
unity of
being
when body,
mind,
spirit
impinge at a
point of
pure
being.

We yearn to keep
this fullness of

contemplation,
but we are
mortal and
slip into the
ways of
every day.

These glimpses
this realization
of the oneness
of life
sustain us.
May we be led
to a repose—
contemplation—
beacon
of the goals
we seek.

Toronto, Canada, June 1973

A WISH . . . TO YOU

As straight toward your goal
as the pointed fir
as firm as the foundation rock
may your spirit emanate
a myrrh
that evokes the best.

May you cause to grow
the precious flower
of sympathy
and for the rest
may the peace
that passes understanding
be yours.

AH, MUSIC!

Ah, music, you are
joy, comfort, solace.
For moments
you transport us
to realms where we sense
beauty, truth, essence
that seep away
as we live and operate
opaquely
in our corporeal
manifestations.

Sad, bowed, discouraged
and alone
we would die
without your
interstices of
light, beauty, goodness.

April 1966

AMIABLE ADVERSARIES
My Trampoline and I

Thrice daily we encounter each other.
There you are—black-faced and resilient
on your four squat legs.
A band of brown plastic
pie-crimped in reverse
encircles you, hiding your
evil-looking coiled springs.

I sit on your center
with legs and feet extended.
One hundred mental counts I bounce.
Then, standing I rise on my toes
only thirty-five times as calves protest.
Next, with feet firmly planted
I bounce in place one hundred times.
Then, one hundred quick jogging steps.
Lastly, I am briefly airborne
one hundred times. Not bad—
not bad for a small woman of 82.

Winter 1982

41

AND DAYS ARE FINITE . . . FINITE

Sometimes, my dear,
it seems my heart must break.
I long for you, long for you.
I think the hardest thing
is to realize that days pass
not to return—
days, weeks, months
that can never be lived with you
and days are finite, finite.

I want you to see what I see
to feel the cooling breeze
to hear the homely rural sounds.
The world though filled
can be a lonely place
without the one you love.

September 1948

ANTICIPATION

My love, my dear,
is coming.
Heart! Be still!
Ear! Harken to
the bells
that ring, ring
in the heady air
of anticipation
of imagination
of memory.

There won't be
words—at first,
but his eyes
will read
my whole
my vulnerable
heart.

At that loved voice
I'll know again
an evanescent
silver joy.
His smallest
touch
will draw me
into a charmed
circle.

A circle
that widens
and widens
to include
the world
the universe
and its name
is love.

October 1946

AT OUR BEST

Why do we
sometimes
know such
well-being
peace
contentment?

It could be genes
the weather
a high moment
of understanding
the perfect synchronization
of our many
"systems"
the evanescent
beauty of
sound
sight
the finishing
of a thing of
beauty
a sudden insight
that loosens
tension.

Too fleetingly
we just ARE
the essence
of us
at our best.

AUTUMN FLOWER

Autumn flower, born of
the deepest richness
of my late garden,
bear your burning beauty
high.
Deep, deep
let me drink
your color
your light
your fragrance
to illumine and
perfume
the thinning air.

Inept gardener
that I was
life slowly taught me
and somehow willed
one late, but glowing
harvest
not profuse
lesser blooms.

Worn are my tools and
strength
but schooled
my patience.

I humbly await
the beckoning glow
of a new
apprenticeship.

AWAKENING IN BEAUTY

Your smile warms the growing cold of my heart.
With your voice the
secret melody mutely felt caresses me.
Loving you I see
intensely subtle color, fresh form, vigorous line.
All about me has palpable third dimension.
Purpose is felt, and with that
a sympathy all but dead surges vitally.
Humility bows my head.
Love brings this awakening in beauty.

August 1936

BARCAROLLE

Play me a barcarolle
grave and slow;
let your fingers liquidly
release the flow of tone on tone.
Comes surcease of pain, and, lo,
as aching poignancy of moan
rises to intensity
well I know
I must attune my soul.

August 1936

50

BE NOT CONFINED

Be not confined in
limited space.
As your lungs
luxuriate in
beneficent air
so your corporeal
being craves
escape.
Let your feet
feel the resilience
of earth; your body
swing in
natural rhythm
unfettered.
Hear all sounds
as though for the
first time.
Really look at the grass
trees and sky;
see the fluid line,
grace of structure,
the gush and
nuance of color.
That large boulder
there ahead
suggests
a rest, but more
a place to think
on these things.

Inanimate though
it seems, it is
living. Could we
but be it, we would
feel time—or rather
we would be
so very old we would
feel eternal.
We would recognize
no seven ages
of man but just
BE
expanded consciousness
BE
space, color,
form, rhythm, feeling
BE
forever free
most exquisitely
alive in
all.

Yucaipa, California 1970

BECOME ONE

Lie on the earth
let sift and flow
the myriad meanings
in strange symbols
but terms
your coursing rhythm
recognizes.

The surge of the sea
is in the sough, sough
of the pliant leaves.

There is even the undertow
that haunts a racial memory
to lure us to a completeness
an unremembered clairvoyance.

The warm shaft soothes;
multiple fragrance softly stirs.

Deeply imbibe harmony, peace.
Drift—drift. At last
the earth and you
become one.

BEES IN WILLOWS

Hear the sound of tiny drills
accidentals and trills.
New green willow trees
are a-hum with these
myriads of bees.
Fragrant essence distills
in minute winged sugar mills.

BEREFT

The loved one recedes into shadow;
the dear face dissolves into mists.
Jewelled lights of spirit
dim to amorphous glow.
Steps once lithe, then slow
fashion no decibels.
A voice once so near
stirs no listening void.
Gestures, beloved of form and flesh,
evoked such personal arabesques
the ambient air sighs the loss.

BIRTHDAY

Once more the year has run
its sands, slowly sifting
with the trimestral shifting
in relation to the sun.

The huge hourglass turns and tips
in our autumn's golden haze
as swings the rhythm of our days
the glass too soon from eager lips.

BITTER BLIGHT

Stars of the winter night,
keep unblurred your beauty bright
from sadness' bitter blight.

Blight that gnaws the inner core
of what is born to soar
and soar forevermore.

More light from some warm sun
give this poor plant, or, run
the sap, and life be done.

December 1936

BITTER SALT

My need for you is a shuddering cry
that rends me in the quiet dark;
that passing ambience unaware
of engulfing waves that choke and
bitter salt of love's dead destiny.

In long distant years I foresee
the grasping of
"It is better to have loved, and lost—"
but this night, this day, the
processions that could
be mellow fruitful years
are cold stones of an unlit hearth.

December 1936

BREAK-UP

There is an aloneness
that is devastating.
To remain estranged is
impossible;
to leave, to run away
solves nothing.
The factors of deep
discord
are in my head
where thoughts turn
endlessly.
The dreary facts are
marshalled.
I try to put myself
in your place—
to hear again
nuance of tone
that signalled the
wedge of
disunion.

So I tried, struggled,
wept. How long?
How much time inched its way?
It is useless to
ponder longer.
For now it is as if
to scream across a canyon,

to watch widening water
between ship and shore.

A flame burned
the backward path;
lightning rent
the habitat of
understanding;
thunder crashed
fragile supports;
cruel and bitter words
were the final
destroyers of our
marriage.

April 1971

BRIDGES

What a magic word to
recall water, rushing, calm;
a pool, a lake, even a
quiet rivulet.

The first frail effort to reach
a place cut off
by shining water
was as a hand held out
in friendship. Even a
drawbridge was let down
to friends.

Hear a partial litany
in honored roll;
Alexander the Third, Hoogli,
Washington, Waterloo,
Firth, Oakland, Auckland,
London, Galata.

How different bridges are:
suspension, pontoon, cantilever.
Some are low and unrailed.
There are the steeply arched
bridges of Japan,
the weathered covered bridges
of old New England.

At Montreal the big ship
seems to touch the horizontal
bar. The Golden Gate in
name and fame stirs the imagination
and delights the eye.
And, oh, the beauty of the
many bridges over
the Seine. And to think
the Pont Neuf is now the oldest crossing
in Paris.

So, the world around
in wood, stone, steel, concrete
they resound to wheel and step.
The feet halt to rest and
refresh the spirit for
that water down below
always changing yet
ever the same
is hypnotic.

To the desperate it
says, "End it all," but
those who do just that
are few.

What is lovelier
than to see the moon reflected
as silver with rippling darker

bars or the water by sun
bedazzled. Our modern
sun worshippers lie on
banks undisturbed by the
multitudes who in cities
hurry by.

The "real" bridges offer
the prosaic, the unchanged,
but consider the
many bridges of the spirit.
These dispense with
speech, but communicate
subtly.

There are moods of nature
with color, motion, sound;
hues the artist paints
in rhythm of line;
the tones of music;
the textured balance
of sculpture;
the expression of eye
and individuality
of gesture.

Then there is that last
invisible bridge whose
approach we may

sense but
whose terminus is
unknown.

This is the bridge
toward which we
all are traveling
in diverse vehicles
of self richly
garmented
in carriages of state
or poorly clothed
and moved by our
own weary feet.

Be we famous, infamous
or miserably obscure
this crossing is
inevitable
for all.

London, England, July 1970

BRIGHTEST GOLD

Great heaps of brightest gold
were piled on crushed pink velvet.
A hazy blue veil floated—floated.
Was it a dream?
Just sunset today.

Wyoming, July 1939

DESERT DUSK

Dusk settles with gentle wings.
Soft scarves subtly fade.
Pullulating sounds
raise their earnest voices
attesting life.

Mesquite with airy grace
weaves exquisite filigree
against a pearly sky.
The first gold diamond
glitters in the west.

Christmas 1943

DESERT VIGNETTES

Noonday heat and stillness
stillness and noonday heat.
Though soon to gain shelter in a dim retreat
'neath sturdy adobe walls cool and sweet,
stand! stand where you are!
Let the hot piercing needles
reach the inner core
of your sensitivity.

Go out. Step into the cool freshness
that follows the searing heat.
Watch the last long shadows in unhurried retreat
behind the relentless line of bold mountain
that against pale yellow curtain knows no defeat.

Spring 1936

DESERT RHYTHM

In constant palpable motion
the wind is tearing at the desert trees.
With sand and dust the air is heavy.
An eerie grayness is the night
for the moon is quite quite new.

To sense this ageless rhythm
man must be all alone
and sheltered from the harsh rush
of abrasive sand;
must know respite
for philosophic measure
of his environment.

He must love it, if he can
but perforce, come to terms with it.
There can be no subterfuge;
only stark truth avails;
but from confrontment comes harmony.

April 1938

DON JUAN

Another face, a new allure
leads you on.
I wish I could be sure
you would retrace
your steps and not detour
around my waiting heart.

Foolish you, easily deceived!
Simple man.
Always searching bereaved
missing what you seek
not knowing love retrieved
is subtle comfort.

March 1938

EACH OF US IS RESPONSIBLE

If peace must first
be in the hearts of
men
then war now occupies
that traditional seat
of compassion.

Nothing is as sad
as to know
that each of us is
responsible
for the horrors of
this era
from the beginning
of this most
ignoble of wars—
this blight and
ruthless
destruction of
Viet Nam
then Cambodia and
Laos.

Fine words of
"freeing the people"
mask
vicious greed and
lust for power.

We "free" them to
death
death by napalm
bullet
grenade
machine gun.
We devastate
vast areas.
We burn their villages.
We make millions
refugees.

It is a nice question
as to whether it
is more
depraved
to do to them
what we do
or what we do
to our own people.
Our youth are
brutalized;
made to believe
"ideology"
is more real
than life.

On balance
the wrongs
we have perpetrated

are worse than
what we are doing
to ourselves.
We attack them in their
homeland.

What defiles
the very heaven
is that man
supposedly rational
retreats from all
common sense.

His undisputed technology
is put to
criminal use in
opposition to every
just
kind
humane
response.
Man still knows
justice
kindness
humanity, so
he ultimately
recognizes the
imperative of
confrontation of
evil and good.

Our duality can
no longer
survive.
Man must
envision himself as
whole.
His social and
spiritual evolution
demand this.
No man can be
"whole"
with evil in his
heart.

April 1971

ELEMENTAL LOVERS

The earth kissed the sky
in a firm yet subtle line
while a cloud coterie blushed.
The diminishing sun
burnished the lovers.

ETCH ON YOUR HEART
(Suggested by *Valse* Op 24 No. 1 by M. Moszkowsky)

Could I but erase
the inscrutable face
of impending gloom.
My love foretells
despair—deep wells
to engulf us.

Etch on your heart
in its most secret part
this hour.
In eternal memory
keep this melody
this haunting waltz.

Feel my arms around you, so.
Hear my words so full of woe.
My heart must ever break.
Let the moon in white
the richly studded night
recall our ecstasy.

May this mournful strain
now portending pain
evoke our love.
Then feel my arms around you, so;
hear my words still full of woe;
know my heart must forever
      break   break   break.

                  March 1937

ELSIE'S BIRTHDAY

It is nearly a half year
since you left me.
Many waning and waxing moons
have come and gone.
But your going is final.
Memories live but
are not warm reality.

We on earth are time
conscious.
The past is a tenuous invisible
thread on which
we hang events
and feelings—disordered
and disproportioned
as they likely are.
The present is a
breath become past.
The future is the most
uncertain of all.

As for death
we on earth cannot possibly
know what you are
or experience.

On this mortal sphere
today is
your birthday.
It would be your eighty-third.
For forty-six of these many years
we made it YOUR day
as it should be—for our birth
marks our emergence as a
part of the human race.

Yet each becomes "I"
different from every
other mortal, yet
by his humanity, perceptive
of the bond
that unites us
despite rents,
burns, discolorations
in the fabric of our
mutuality.

Spring seems early and warm
this year.
Were you here, you would
be having flowers planted
to watch them day by
day.

I sit in the afternoon
warmth
and miss you
miss you.

It is good to believe that
you as spirit
can no longer suffer
as you did
in your physical body.

You were locked
in a frame
of limited mobility;
yet your mind
roamed the world.
Your concern was for all
and especially for me
who was your friend
always at hand
for nearly a
half century.

So, I think of you
on this
your natal day
and love you.

February 27, 1975

78

FAIR DREAM

(Suggested by Debussy's *Clair de Lune*)

To wake from a dream
of one so fair
is to know
hurt unassuaged.
Soft the air
where moonlight mist
bejewelled your dusky hair.
No sapphire stars
could dim your pellucid eyes.
My trembling hand
dared to trace
the delicate heart shape
of your face.
Your mien
was utter grace.
Dulcet clear tones
said tender words to me.
Memories like moans
tear my heart.
Without you
what am I?
A soul apart.
You are perfume
on a haunting strain
a tender touch
on a mortal hurt.
I can only live
to dream.

FANTASY

In the dark and quiet hours
when sleep finds not
my weary body
and troubled mind,
unrelated memories
make fantastic
swatches
of varied colors
and fanciful
weaves—
patterns bold
flash to
fashion
new insights.

Sudden tropical
dark
is streaked by
"northern lights"
of my youth.

Flutey sounds
and horns
come from
temples of
eastern isles.

Raucous caws
in sultry land
are followed by
the meadow lark's
sweet song.

Bamboos tall
in clustered cloud
are succeeded by
rustling pliant
leaves of corn.

The self-same wind
that moires the sea
waves the prairie grain.

The apple green on
lovely tree
colors in segment
small the
sunset sky
after the brighter
rosy glory
has fled.

In an island far away
the oxen cart
is time slowly paced

even as the eyeless bird
flashes the
vault
reaching, reaching—
to distances
we cannot
imagine.

My heart patiently
pulsing
is somehow
akin to the
movement of the
spheres.
One rhythm is as
easy to understand
as the other.

A cry of pain
near at hand
synthesizes
all pain.
We can even
not hear
the sound at our side
nor feel the shudder
of our brother.

What hope of
heeding the
more distant cry?

The need that is
near
must be deep and
clear to our hearts and
minds
if we are to rise to a
height to
see the picture whole.

The color
the shape
the scale complete
the touch
the taste
all must meet
in the center
of each
to bring to
birth our
human
divinity.

Ceylon (Sri Lanka) 1970

FIRE

There is something in me
that loves fire.
Of course I do not mean
the destruction
it can do,
but I like the gentle gleam
in a fireplace
or when winds howl
and cold sweeps in
it can roar to our
satisfaction.

I like to lay a fire—to
put in paper
pile in kindling
then light wood
to easily catch
then sturdy chunks
for longer burning.

But one must not
forget a fire.
It demands substance
to provide heat
and soft light
when switches are off.

It is not discriminating;
it will consume
anything. Fling it
your apple peelings and cores,
candy wrappers,
old letters,
old notebooks,
shopping lists,
worn-out handbags,
catalogs that
crowd our mail,
cardboard boxes that
brought unexpected gifts,
milk cartons that
sputter as they
burn.

"This end up" and
"Handle with care"
give off
lovely ruby
green and blue
flames, as do
catalogs, too, with
their garish pictured
offerings.

Late at night
yawning, still
we linger
bewitched by
the breathing coals.

In the morning
ashes deceive us.
When we toss into
this capacious basket
crumpled paper,
it lies on
the soft bed of ashes
and then briefly flares.
We can, if we will, easily
coax into life
another fire.

Just so in our
own lives
what seems
cold and remote
memory or
chance encounter can
bring to brightness
and evoke
to live again
that which had left us.

December 1975

FJORD-SUMMER NIGHT

Blue fuses with gray pearl
where headlands nearly meet.
Softly rounded hills are covered
with pines individually picoted
against a pale sky.

No lonely landscape this.
Sturdy little houses charm, and
one feels a dignity that holds
itself not cheaply. The Viking
spirit lives.

Near coast of Norway, June 1937

FLIGHT

April with tear-stained face
dark scowls erased by sylphan grace
of gleeful laughter
who looks not before nor after
come! come away with me
to unmapped land, uncharted sea.

Teach me to shed all sham
to reach full stature, be as I am.
There let me labor with a will
imbued with pride and skill
unwanted in technocracy
still threaded by hypocrisy
but, mostly, let my senses glow
let this anachronism know
the treasures unsurpassed.

Unsuspecting man in his forte
never tastes the flavor
the subtle provocative savor
of uninhibited living
for freely giving
tears and laughter with consummate grace
to April with the tear-stained face.

December 1936

FOREIGN CEMETERY

It is old, very old
grey and harsh.
The tombs ranged
above the earth
unconsciously accept
the rain, the heat,
the winds that blow
from the nearby sea and
monotonous plain.

The cypress tall
compact and
darkly green
somberly points
to that other world
that we,
knowing it is unknown,
still picture as above the
blue.

Grandfather, and before him
his grandfather,
was lovingly laid here
to rest;
then grandmother
and their children, too.

Close are neighbors
their blood lines
inextricably mixed.
There are strangers
with odd sounding
names
barely visible—
wayfarers whose silver cord
was broken
far from home.
An occasional
prayer
for them is said by
a loving soul
whose compassion
reaches to all.

The vineyards all about
reborn each welcome Spring
brightly assert
life that knows no end—
life that springs from
what dead did seem.
The cycles are without end.

One senses
with wonder
and sadness

that, while life is eternal,
he, though he lives
life today,
will soon
not see
the greening vine
the blue above
the cypress tall
nor hear
the wind
the singing bird.
He, too, will
unconscious
lie
among his
people.

St. Laurent d'Aigouze, France 1967

FROM MY WINDOW

My view is a little square giving precious air,
the green of trees, a vagrant breeze.
Pigeons inquisitive, on their initiative
perch on my window sill, preen their feathers at will,
promenade pompously, then fly ponderously
to dispute a narrow perch, only suddenly to lurch
    aloft.

Their chorus of a morning is dolorous;
I wonder why their song ends all wrong.
The listener is committed to want that last note
    omitted.
Other smaller birds sing gaily, happy among the trees
that gamely affront the apartments' bare walls
within which are some rooms like stalls.

When I arrived, the chestnut tree
with glorious clusters among the leaves
made bouquets—some white, some pink.
One knew it was Spring and could think
of other places long left behind
where life was less confined.

I see roofs in uneven incline with chimney pots in
    line.
Now they are useless and cold, but
in winter their smoke will cut
the sky—sometimes blue but more often grey

showing that down below fire has a way
to give warmth and cheer.

Now that summer is here
I see the sunset glow on windows that throw
back colors, and the sky scarce darkens by
the time the morning sun will peek
over the rim. Early many will seek
by hurry and work to maintain
the body of the city and its brain
that its people flourish and live to nourish
the spirit of this city, peerless, wonderful
precious Paris.

Paris 1970

FRUITING TREE

Fruiting tree,
you bring plums to me
plump and lush
with purple blush.
Your delectable juice
sugared, does produce
a nectar to delight
the taste and sight.

As I sip and savor, I see
in my mind, a graceful tree
aglow with small
white flowers, not at all
aware of fruit to come
just being a staggering sum
of petals small, frosting on tree.
Yet, how can that be?
To glisten against sky so blue
it just can't be true.
But, yet, it exists,
in memory. It persists.

May it ever be so
that beauty and glow
live in our hearts
till life departs.

Yucaipa, June 1972

GLOOM

Gloom hung from his shoulders
as he stood there
by the granite boulders
heavy with the years
brought from God knows where.

In his eyes were dimming tears
to blind his sight
turned inward to his fears.

All was ugly; nothing, fair
in this distorted light.
Sharp spears slashed and ghoulish leers
lashed his despair.
Gloom hung from his shoulders.

August 1936

95

GOOD-BYE

For this long good-bye
let me hold you to
my wretched heart.
Beauty and love so
precious
I would I could
have you forever.

Lovely serene fair brow
fronting a fine clear
mind; eyes of
flawless beauty
that gently probe to
my very core of being,
that bless with
understanding.

Tender cheeks are
faintly hollowed by
some lurking enemy.

And oh, my love, my heart,
the sweet curve of
a mouth that melts all
doubt and wrong and woe
and bears in its breath
promise of immortality.

September 1938

GROWTH

In what diverse ways
comes change.
The hidden seed
bursts its capsule
and is well started
before the plant
first pushes into
view.

Bare trees begin
to green slowly
then burgeon
into full form and
color.

How eagerly in
northern land
we await the
first buds and
flowers of Spring.

Flowering and
fruition have
naturally
symbolized
spiritual
growth.

From aeons of
reappearance
of the flowers
of Spring we
see beauty in
the autumn
though
it portends
latency.

We don't know what
seeds are in us
implanted.
General nurture
and health
can fairly well
assure an
average garden,
but
dark circumstance
can invade us;
black shadow
obscure the
usual sun of
our lives.
Discord vanquishes
harmony;
roughness
bruises our
vulnerability;

jagged stem
pierces us;
rapier thrusts
draw blood.

We would hide
in some deep
crevice
our lacerated
bodies and
broken
spirits.
We are spent
survivors of
personal
shipwreck.

Yet, to live
seems paramount.
We can't quit
this life in
despair.
Somewhere are
sun and the
warmth
of human touch
to lead us
back to
living.

In some day
long past
our compassion
left in us a
will to
growth,
a durable seed
that awaited
this dark
hour,
dreary cold,
and desolation
to attest the
permanence
of sun and
rain and
soil to
nurture
new
growth.

May 1971

HEALING

Deep in my soul
a yearning
knows surcease
when healing
music
brings release
in tears.

Purity of tone
invades
aching sadness
that pervades
me;
transforms grayness
to light.

Poignant joy
singled
from sound divine
is mingled
glory
to enshrine
my soul.

December 1944

HILLS OF MEXICO
(Tamazunchale)

Uplifted fecund-breasted hills
pointed with verdant maize
that deeply distil substance
from hidden source
that golden grain
sustain earth's most febrile seed.

Man seeks the eternal matrix
that from him may burgeon
more perfect fruit.

Mexico 1935

I AM GRATEFUL

In softened light I have
just listened to Grieg's
Peer Gynt Suite. I lay in
stretch-out comfort and
gave myself to sound.
Not for me activity
with background
music. It could
just as wonderfully have
been Beethoven, Bach,
or a dozen others.

I make music, too,
just for me. The piano
is my instrument. The joy
it brings is something beyond
the sound and pattern.
There is a definite pleasure
my muscles know. The
execution itself
satisfies a need that is
deep and completely
personal.

The fleeting colors of
dawn and
sunset
partly compensate for

103

the harsh realities
we daily face.

Is there anything
more tender than
Spring's first
burst of green?

My heart has
been touched
by my cat's trusting
relaxed response
and confidential expectation
of food and love.
A dog's devotion
is beautiful to
know.

On a bright day
to see the blue above
and changing clouds is to take
heart against
trouble.

An understanding look
a cheery word
a letter from
a friend
are part of my life.

For all this
and more
I am
grateful.

September 1970

I AM THE VINE

I am the vine.
Deep rooted
in blood built soil
I tap the fecund
earth.
Suddenly cut back
each year
I burgeon.
Take—take the
fruit
of quiescent and
active days.

June 1938

I KNOW A MAN

I know a man
a lonely one.
He lives in a world
of books.
His mind is good
there is a cold glow.
Of great poetry
he asks, "Isn't this
ungrammatical?
Though I suppose
a great poet
can do it."
His is a sardonic
thin humor, merciless.
Rages rise quickly
and then danger
lurks in his long arms.
Intuition senses
cruelty clothed
in Christian meekness;
a sadism forged
on God knows what anvil
of despair.
On the clear winter air
I hear his high thin voice
singing, singing the hymns
learned sixty years ago
before life
somehow proved too much.

November 1943

I, TOO, AM A PART

If my soul
were as constant
in varying
motion
as you, O Sea,

If my yesterday
were today
and today
a certain
tomorrow,

If my life were
always beauty
in storm
in peace
in eternity,

I'd know
what God and Man are.

Dreary moaning
gulls
of past mistakes
would not mar
my serenity.

The burning sun
of fires
futilely banked
would no longer
sear.

The moon's clean silver
soothes
the hasty heart
and quiets
the restless mind.

Of the cosmos
I, too, am a part.
Somehow
I am
darkness and light
and constant
inconstant sea.

Ensenada, Mexico 1937

IN PRAISE OF MY WIFE

You are my love
my joy and grace.
Your clear penetrating
look reaches my
most elusive thought.
I am drawn to you
as to a magnet
yet know I am free
to be myself.
I can go off alone
knowing that
when I return
no critical
word or glance
will reproach me.

I can interrupt you
at any task and
not be rebuffed. You will
be attentive when
I say, "Listen to this"
and read something
I wanted to share with you.
It is easy to
lure you to
enjoy lovely
music. The
unexpected sudden

suggestion to
go for a picnic
is met with
warmth. Straightway
you have a hamper ready.

You are quick to
laugh and equally
sensitive to
sympathize
with a
somber mood.
But you are not
weak nor
a reflection of me.

I know well
that no one
fathoms your depths.
Nothing can alter the
inner core
and beauty
of your being. It is
surely formed
of light ineffable
depth impenetrable
gentleness and love.

Paris, Summer 1970

INFINITELY SMALL—INFINITELY LARGE

Our immediate world
we know intimately is finitely small,
but our minds can reach
and encompass more than we know.

This reach somehow sunders us.
The unity we sense
dwarfs our egos, so dear to us.

We are the grains of sand on the shore,
the smallest leaf on the tree,
a drop of dew on the blade of grass.

We must accept a larger purpose.
Severally and individually
we become the strand,
the tree,
the rain,
the continents,
the forest,
the oceans.
The concept expands.
We are a tiny bit of the cosmos.

INSCRUTABILITY

The prow cuts the mobile medium
of the aqueous pathless main.
The wound quickly closes
and infinite inscrutability
claims its own.
Forever the toys of man
have marked their fugitive flight
unknown but for memories
recorded in wood and stone
burial remnants from afar
to placate ancient gods.
This stupendous element
knows no restraint.
Its mighty stirrings destroy.
There is majesty in a wreck
and ever its calms invite.
Struggling and buffeted
a ship may in an unknown port
find harbor. So man
may spend his little force
where he intended not.
The toys of man
and man himself
wound the mobile medium.
His puny thrust quickly closes
and inscrutability claims its own.

On the Atlantic, June 1937

JILTED

You no longer love me, you say?
It's strange, my heart to behave this way.
There have been days and days
in hundreds of ways
you've shown me you felt as I did—
that there was joy in our love, hid.
But now, it seems it was but dreams.

I'm not to know then the sweet words
that flowed from your pen—the
low muted call of your lips from
the garden wall? I'm never to recapture
in your dear arms, rapture?

So, I'm to see you once in a while, but
never to know that intimate, tender smile.
You are sorry, but I'll love someone else again
in this big wide world of available men.

Then, that's all it meant to you?
Well, my dear, that being the case, I'm through.

June 1935

LICHTENSTEIN

I saw a shining castle
high upon the hill.
I climbed and climbed
but did not reach it still.

The bell I pulled and pulled
at the ancient gate;
but seeing the hoary man
did patiently await.

He showed me vaulted cellars
where stores and men were locked
now dark and dull and damp
and my heart with pity nearly stopped.

In a tiny inner court
warming with gentle sun
figments in quaint old dress
and mien did play and run.

My fingers lingered
on the deeply carved panels
my eye measured the heavy beams;
frescoes dim preserved the annals.

The tiny panes
were most cunningly devised
and drew me to the window
where, far beneath, I descried

A narrow street with houses neat
sheer below the castle wall
miniature beings, sheep, oxen, cattle,
horses, dogs-all.

My glance did lift
to patchwork fields and trees
making motley patterns
mellow pleasant panoplies.

I glimpsed the course
of the mighty, mighty Rhine
still beyond I saw the mountains
towering over little Lichtenstein.

Vaduz, quaint capital,
Hail to thee!
May your people pursue their gentle way
undaunted and forever free.

Vaduz, Lichtenstein, September 1938

LIFE IS A LOOM

Life is a loom on which to place
design neither use nor sorrow can efface.
Time controls this game of shuttlecock
that weaves line on line, block on block
with colors so true they will not erase.
The thing you are, your character, your grace
determine the pattern, fill the space
though threads may tangle and stubbornly lock.

Life is a loom.
If the warp be firm,
lost woof just living will replace.
With shuttle, warp and woof, and face to face
with necessity, there can be no mock
of what is fashioned under the shock
of stupendous forces of the human race.

Life is a loom.

LONGING

Longing stretches the
very sinews; speaks with
incisive voice;
courses and writhes with
the mystic stream;
tears the breath that
bears the beloved's name;
blinds the eyes in
sharp solution;
for to love is to suffer.

LOOKS

A girl may be good;
she may be clever.
In the family it may be
she for whom they shout.
But everywhere else—
theater, shop, and round
about—if she is not
a beauty
does it matter?
Ever!

June 1935

MAN, THOUGHTS ON

I have at hand a big book
LEWIS AND CLARK
PIONEER NATURALISTS.
They started out little
knowing what to expect.
New plants they discovered
and animals, too.
The magnificent expanse
in the west
overwhelmed them.
From vantage high
they beheld boundless
reaches of land
soon to know the
restless pioneer
whom nothing
daunted.
He would plow and sow
and reap and build.
Many moved
hurried ever onward
and westward
until the sea
stopped their headlong
course.
Decades and decades—
more than a century
passed.

Now the great expanses are
becoming too populated.

The earth will not be
raped with
impunity. Its denizens
dwindle. Impure air,
noise and presence
of man bring
beasts low. They
sicken and die.
Once bright, water now
is lethal. Man progresses
but leaves in his wake
evils both tangible and
impalpable.
In his grasping course
man negated the spirit
and made substance
his goal.
He ravished
the good earth
which, nurtured
lovingly, his seed—
children, grandchildren,
descendants on, on, on,
could have cherished.
But febrile man
has chosen
the quick return

the diminution
of his fellows.
What cares he
for the flesh
and spirit
of those who fall
even his own?
Worse, the powerful
with machinations
promote war.
Juggling of figures,
talk of parity
and overkill,
and "safe" levels
of poison
deceive the people.
The unthinking respond
to demagoguery and
chauvinism.
They are filled with fear.

Somehow, many men
have lost their
dignity—the sense
of what it is to be
human.
Masses are numbers
to be manipulated
expertly. But
the positive good

deep embedded
still protests evil. It
awaits the clarion
call to surge
anew
to build a life
of harmony for
us all.

February 1971

MOON LURE

A glow comes before.
    Red disk of tremendous size—
above the sculptured hills, arise!
    Before thy charmed gaze
let us again amaze
    remembering your changing lovely lore.

White pale mistress of the skies
    that lures to madness
that imparts a sadness
    limpid lady of the night
with starry jewels bedight,
    do you believe the ardor in men's eyes?

Though high, high above
    you ride serene
cold and lifeless, so they say,
    how is it . . . pray . . .
that hearts beat faster
    voices have sweet laughter
a lad to his lass doth lean
    'neath the willow screen
and much is made of love?
    and much is made of love?

December 1935

MORNING

Morning sun,
arise over each segment
of your earth.

Light with clarity
men's tenebrous
minds.

May men see clearly
the still bounteous
earth;
the embracing
seas
with their
fruitful promise.

Let the myriads of
men
longing to live
as
brothers
be not balked
in their transcendent
desire
by forces of
darkness that threaten
attack
whisper deceit

mouth lies
hold on high
emblems of
arms.

Believers in
love of man
convinced of this
healing and lifting
power of
compassion
give outpourings
of strength
help and
love
to fashion
a world of
brotherhood
to bring a
new day.

MOUNTAINS

You surround, enclose
and cherish me. So, I feel you.
You are near—to the East
gently rounded only
a brief buffer to the
morning sun.

Your surface is harsh, rocky
nearly barren
spotted with
juniper.

Three great windows
of the home that shelters me
present views
to expand one's being.

To the North
is a commanding dark line
against the blue
of day. When there is
moonlight, it is
silvered to mystery.

The slope upward
is steady, leading the eye
to the height.
No foothills lessen
majesty of ascent.

Foreground junipers
are darkly green.

There is no house
in view. There are
just mountains
sky and you.

Before night lowers
rosy light colors
the earth that loses
the beneficent
sun that hurries
to awaken
others like me.

Then night with
its softness and
soothing dark and
arms of earth
protect me so
I do not feel the
universe
too heavy
upon me.

And tomorrow
and tomorrow
tomorrow
the ageless
rhythm.

Pearblossom, California 1972

MY ETERNAL JOY

My love's smallest caress
is enough to bless
me forever.
Forget it? Never!

Her mouth a coral curve
replete with charm and verve;
her eyes' clear glowing gaze
wins one a hundred ways.

Her chin has a tilt
to make a suitor wilt
her burnished hair, a maze
I'll follow always.

This lovely confection
of my predilection
is quite without alloy
and my eternal joy.

MY HEART YEARNS

My heart yearns
to tell its love.
You, so far away!
My cry is crushed.
No strong wind can carry it.
I cannot touch you;
I cannot see you;
neither do I hear
the voice my coveting ear
strains to catch.
I would be desolate,
but memory brings
you close. But not
close enough.
Do you recall?
And don't you remember?
Oh, yes, so many things.
The day we walked in the rain
(but our fused suns made rainbows).
The idle hours on the placid lake;
the strenuous climb to vantage peak;
the campfire at close of day;
the muted call of feathered friends;
the solemn march of the stately moon;
the music that stirs and twists the heart;
the poems of life and love
(and so of you and me)—
That is it! Life and love—
they *are*—for you and me.

September 1945

MY NEIGHBOR'S MULES

My neighbor's boss has a new pair of mules
"They are marvelous fine," says he to me.
"Five hundred they must have cost, or more,
and you'll hunt long before
you find their like."
Tonight on taking a hike
to cut arrow weed to make a fence,
I heard . . . . comments!
as he was plowing
the stubborn soil.
The mules (marvelous fine beasts, as he said to me)
appeared to be
aloof and uninterested
in lowly toil.
In short, they did not want to foil
their spirits—wanted to be free.
I'd hate to spend
five hundred or more
on marvelous fine beasts
that foreswore
the work they were intended for.
Late tonight, the struggle over
the one to his bed
the other, clover
I wonder what the cogitations be
and, if offered—say-five hundred—or more, well—
if he'd sell.

June 1936

131

MY PLUM TREE

From my window at midnight
a late October moon looks down.
Your closely clustered limbs
cast a dark circular shadow.
Rising high your
still abundant leaves
glint frostily
in lunar light.

During shortening autumn and
winter days, gentle and harsh
winds will shear away
your crown.
There will come about
a new beauty of sculptured
structured form
giving rise to stark outline
against sunny
winter skies and intriguing
shadows on the earth beneath.

Spring will clothe
the tree in delicate white
beauty of blossom.
Then, hardly perceived at first,
her dress becomes
tender green.

Lengthening summer days
bring forth tiny green plums
that expand and become
plump and purple.
Their texture and taste
are perfect. The harvest is
beautiful bounty.

The cycle is complete as I gaze
with wonder at the heavily
leaved plum tree
glowing in moonlight
outside my window.

October 1982

MY TIGER BLANKET

I love my tiger blanket
so thick and soft and warm
of "lana pura" of the llama
it is made,
and it came from far Peru,
the City of the Kings.

Graceful cats stalk across its borders
upon some expedition bent
fearlessly I snuggle them to my neck
relax and read.

Dark and tawny mottlings
in careless folds
keep me snug and warm
while I browse and drowse
in jungles real, vicariously,
or, fascinated, gaze upon
the jungles of my fellow man.

I love my tiger blanket
from the City of the Kings.
Let's have tigers ruthlessly pursue
through anachronistic jungles
the rapacity of man.

March 1938

NIGHT IS COME

Delphinium blue fills
the angles of the rugged thrusts.
Out of sight, the Phoebus, by reflected might,
colors in amethystine light
the tooled oriental hills.
Creeping velvet black lusts
to enfold the recumbent sun.
Twilight dies; night is come.

August 1936

NORTH ATLANTIC PASSAGE

A greyish charcoal smudge
    is Newfoundland.
A leaden oily sea
    against the icy peaks
discloses aquamarine.
    Mystery is the key
of an iceberg;
    solitude, the motif.

June 1937

OF PALM AND PINE

On tropic strand the graceful palm leans
away from its mother, land.
The constant trades that blow with tireless force
have caused it so to grow.
How different in the North, the pine
that towers with dignity
rises in majestic vertical line.
With brothers in countless number
in their fraternity, during the winter
there is apparent slumber.
Deep damp snow
covers the world at their feet
and all is quiet whiteness below.
Fierce summer elements
rock even their firm stand
but alter scarce at all their lineaments.
White flashes blind their lofty gaze;
thunderous din wounds their mighty ears;
but, with the lull, they grow their ordained ways.
If disaster come, some noble weal
and massive limbs dissever,
the kingly tree knows its wounds to heal.
Though time and mischance may mar its face,
a gash may even reach its heart—
there it stands, faithful to its place.
Of palm and pine, one is no more noble than the
    other;
each must yield to circumstance
and obedience to its laws discover.

OH, MOON! OH, SUN

Even as I write
on this paper in the light
of my lamp, I feel the
force of you, Oh, Moon!
I do not sleep undisturbed
when you look down in full
effulgence.

I leaned on my window sill
drinking in your magic light.
Your light is as
powerful
over us as that brighter one
of your brother
the sun.

You entice us to greater heights
of consciousness.
In the glare of noon
we dismiss the
fantasies of the
night.

We are conditioned to be
"practical"—
to see the world "as it is"—that
"black is black and white is white."
Everything is in sharp outline,

and can't we see what is so
plain before us?

Some of us rebel against
this harshness and
remember the softness
of the moonlight with
its glow and the
mysterious depth of
black shadow.

The light of these
heavenly orbs somehow
invades us—seeks
our core of
being
to our anguish and our
joy.

We are divided.
Only in moments
do we master the balance
that makes us
whole.

Maybe this tension
is to bring us
in fusion to a
perception of
perfection.

August 1974

139

OH, MOON
(Written antecedent to the "moonwalk.")

Don't you ever fret and gloom,
oh, unknown, aloof, cold Moon?
Aren't you sometimes weary?
Don't you ever feel dreary
from eternally waxing and waning
and stability never attaining—
and the ebb and flow
of your oceans here below?
Do you ever have attacks of
conscience
or, are you lax
in cosmic matters?
Do you know the rags and tatters
of stratagem?
Do you have a ferocious boss
whose goal is gain or loss?
Are you just a hired man
doing your job the best you can?
I can keep on asking
questions like these
and answer just as I please.
After all, I am glad you
ride so high
guarding your mystery in
the sky.

OH, NIGHT

The trees are too dark a
silhouette
against the lighter sky.
The wind weirdly twists
their supple arms reaching
reaching to what?

The full moon
lights the open glades.
But to what purpose?

The night sounds
rise and subside.
Their minor cadence
burdens the heart
with sorrow.

The night
brings dark hours
when sadness dares drop
the mask of hope—
dares embrace
the bright illusion
of a dream.

Oh, night!
Bring sleep and rest
and surcease of longing.

August 1946

141

OPEN WINTER

Thin golden leaves
suffused obliquely
by morning sun
are precious coins
early spent by any
vagrant flurry.

Behold some now
in tarnished heaps
that rustle
with the passing
of tiny creatures.

Come Spring rains
dulled gold becomes
richness, earthy mould
to nourish
a splendor of flowers.

Every plant bursts
into fragile green;
again it is Spring.

OR LET ME DIE

It has come—a loss
so great that it numbs.
Words that would comfort
ricochet from impassivity.
Yes, yes, of course I must go on.
That is what SHE would want.
That brave and tender spirit
would grieve
to know its passing
created irreparable pain.
Life forms change
and those we knew
we know no more.
But they, they must surely
pass to embracing compass
of things and beings here.
Only thus can I bear
the unkind things I did
the words too quickly spoken
the irritation not
suppressed.
Oh, dear one, beyond the
emptiness that gives no echo
even of emptiness,
somehow reach me,
or let me die.

OUR CHESTER, THE CAT

This crisp morning you lie
a furry, flattened ball.
Your striped tail
with ebony tip
is snugly, tightly,
curved lovingly
around the cushion of
you, delicately covering
your nose and mouth.
By show standards you are
an alley cat
brindle striped. Your fur
is not long, but thick
and you always smell
deliciously clean.
Your eyes are clear and
bright.
Your mouth is in a generous
patch of white as is your
immaculate short vest.
No cat could have
neater white feet.
And your toes—three on
each foot are white
the fourth like the rest of
your tigerish coat.
You climb onto my sister's lap
at every opportunity.
She is often at her desk,

and from frequent occurrences
of being lifted down,
you now groggily
leave her lap
when the telephone rings
only to resume your place
to lie happily or sleep.
Now, though quite sedate,
often you race over the grass
or run wildly
from room to room.
You like company, and
when guests come,
you curl up or stretch out
in the center of the room
and are likely, too,
to leap on the back of a chair
on which someone sits.
Perhaps your name should be
Greg for
gregarious.
By human aging, you
are now a hundred five years old
but who would believe it!
Knowing the inevitable,
we enjoy and love
you each passing day
and hope you will be
our cherished love
for long.

August 1978

PAIN

Pain endows its own
harsh school. Each one
sooner or later
enters its portals.
Pain may come in
shuddering gasps
that rend the body and
dismay the spirit;
or, its slow grip
of terror
rises and rises to
agony.
What does one do
again and again?
Endures.

January 1968

146

QUIETUDE

Listen to the gentle
song of unseen bird;
catch the effortless flow
of luminous insect;
move with the slowly changing
shadow
cast by the westering sun
across the oriental garden
of your rug;
sense the monotonous two-four
beat in sage tone
of your ancient clock;
the varying burnish
of its
pendulum.

Of course, it marks
time—
your time diminishing.
But be not concerned
for now you live
in consciousness
of all that is.
Touch with sensuous memory
the smooth stone of
your most precious
ring.

Hear again the promise
when it was given.
Lift your face to
enveloping mist of
mountain glen
when everything was
excluded
and you were alone
in an alien world.

Revel in the light
of a refulgent moon
that so imbues familiar things
that you can see them
with expanded
interiority
permanence
beauty.

Reread with wonderment
the poetry of giants.
Therein is a reality
that synthesizes
the deepest flashes of
your being, those
moments
when consciousness
reaches its
eternal essence
and home.

May 1971

RAIN

Ah, rain, rain!
What different faces
you show to us mortals
here below.

So gentle, soft
so fine
the sun
yet makes you shine.

Then, again,
in slashing fierce
lashes
you cut and spill
in noisy rill
down rushing
drain.

The soddened loosened
banks
crash with
roar
to valley
floor.

In torrent wild
destruction's child
you tear at

resistant roots
to topple
great trees,
to dislodge
embedded rock,
to snatch
helpless beast
and puny
man
to whom
anger and
prayer are
vain
to stay your
senseless havoc.

In wanton rage you
release
the tanks of
heaven.

Winds lull.
The sun sends
fingers of light
to dispel the
storm
and dares to
smile at
destruction's
wake.

Auckland, New Zealand, December 1969

150

REST MY FAINTING HEART

Let me lay my head on your breast to rest.
With your arms close around me it is best
to forget the short hours are not forever
and not to think what love could be together.
Your gentle hand smooths my hair—
soothes the dull and dismal care
that with fear would drag my soul to defeat.
But I have your sustaining love replete
with compassionate tenderness. So rest
my fainting heart on your dear breast.

August 1936

RETURN

Somehow I'd have you know
the joy your thoughts
have brought. The glow
that stirs the heart
and seeps into every fiber
until none is unwarmed—apart.

Our lives are prisms
to catch and hold the lovely light
reveal inspiring visions.
We are taut strings
to vibrate to music
of glory: all life that sings.

If we listen a-right
we should hear a surge
of gentle might.
Power that waits
for man, for you and me, to grasp
the immortal gates
to fling them wide.
In life's ceaseless sea
all may forever abide.

June 1945

SEPTEMBER

(On the SS Delmundo, enroute to Argentina)

Now in the September of my years
I groan for the paltry fears
that kept me locked
and blocked
with gray insubstantiality
abundant glorious reality.

Why didn't I grasp
with careful but relentless clasp
the glowing moth-dusted moments
to mosaic in luminance
the substance—the urge
that lifts above the surge
of the unheeding.

Now in penitent kneeling
I pray for a long September
that I may store to remember
glowing opalescent days
caught in long slanting rays.

Oh, help me to be
brave and free
fearless and tearless
to the end.

September 1940

Silence is a bell waiting to sound
in Time's long skein wantonly unwound.

SINCE MY LOVE I CANNOT KNOW

Since my love I cannot know,
give me solace in lesser things—
this sun to warm my blood of painful flow.
Let its glow light my
dark soul's recesses
that hungrily wait—hopelessly
the beneficent touch
of love's caresses.

May warm light rain
gently soften
the stubborn glebe
of pain
so there can rise
vital verdant grass
to nurture others' loves
happier and not destined to pass
into oblivion . . . as does mine.

Christmas 1946

SNOWFALL

Softly sifting
thickening flakes
blur the wooded silence.
A new-made print
is coolly overlaid.

SOUNDS

Is there, or is there not
a slight crepitation
that makes silence
not quite total?

A quarter of a mile
away
cars and trucks
speed along
with varying sound
as though in flight
from some
pursuing
demon.
A slight rise enforces
more power and
often
a shift of gear.
Sometimes there
is an uneven
hurried
beat of
ONE, two
ONE, two.

Too frequently
the strident

shriek
of sirens
splits the
air.
Someone is in
trouble, or maybe
he isn't, but dead
to all.
He is merely
a statistic
among thousands
who overtook
recklessly, or
drove while
sleepy, or
was the victim
of some other
driver's fault.

Farm machinery
clanks and
clonks along
a reminder that
we still depend
on the earth for
existence.

Overhead the
planes, when high,
pulse faintly.

A crop duster will
rattle your
windows.
Your heart lodges
in your throat,
as its stabbing
sound
vibrates close
to your roof.

The coyotes' weird
bark,
rarer each year,
is welcome to my
ears as
symbolic of a
quieter, less
crowded scene.

In my desert
you may hear
the dry croak
of the
road runner.

When young, I
knew the
whispering of
the corn. Who
has heard that

does not
forget it.

When snow is soft,
it deadens
sound, but there
is a stage
when it has a
pleasant
crunch
under foot.

While he may
wake you,
the rooster's
alarm is
welcome to
the rural
dweller.

Your dog's welcoming
bark
is good to hear.
His warning at
other times
reassuring.

Is there a more
peaceful
sound than your

cat's purr as
he rests so
contentedly
on your lap?

Air in motion
can gently
switch a
branch against
your window.
At times there
is the ominous
roar of high wind
that threatens
to rip off the
roof.
Then one waits for
less violent
intervals
with relief
and hopes for
the more
normal sounds.

Rain can be so
gentle it is
soundless
as well as
to beat the
earth with
spats.

Floods
have a
terrifying
roar as
waters churn
embroiling
all they can
wrenching
limbs, trees,
timbers,
boulders,
helpless beasts
and even
man.

Contrast this
with the
rippling sound
of shallow water
over stones.

There is the
mystery and
meaning in
people's voices.
I wonder if they
are aware of
what they say
by their voices.

How well some
of us
come to know
what voices say.
We live in a
dark world of no
sight.
How grateful
we are for
sounds that
must picture
our world.

November 1971

STORM

Dull the sky.
No blue lightens
the gray.
Heavy drops of rain
aslant
hit the panes with
decisive thrust
to runnel furiously
to ledge whence they
slip to
grass below.
Throaty rumbles of
thunder
speak ominously.
A dazzling zig-zag
of lightning
flash
as thunder
rattles the heavens.
Everything in the
open is
wet, wet, wet.
Some passers-by dash for
cover.
The plastic-coated
manikins
push on.

Cars make
fan fountains.
Their tires hiss
like coiled
serpents.
Right about
to look within.
Of course,
no glow of hearth
in August.
Switching on all
the lights helps
defeat the
gloom.
A cup of good hot
tea
will cheer.
A brilliant Chopin
study or
a Beethoven
sonata
will diminish
the crash
of thunder.
The fire of genius
will brighten the
gloom.

Utah, August 1971

SUFFERING

The bone of my soul
protrudes to bear
the sharp cold thrusts
of attack.
No shroud of
flesh abates
the pain.

SUMMER IN THE DESERT

Summer in the desert?
How terrible they say.
Terrible, yes, but
not from the heat.

Terrible it is in
the intensity of awareness it
arouses.

Be it early,
mid day, or late, there is
a pulsating vitality that
forces all barriers.

Sleep under a giant cottonwood
to awaken in the before mystic dawn
to varied calls and sounds.

Blurred early eyes behold
fugitive feathered shapes.

The acuter ear is tickled
and quaintly brushed by
sounds
bubbling and tumbling and mumbling from
small throats.

Smile with
tenderly curved lips for the
joy of
ear and eye.

Lightly stretch a
body remade
in hours of limpid nothingness
lighted by starlight
caressed by downy-tipped fingers of
the wind.

Stretch and sigh—
to sleep again.

SUNSET

Sunset like sunrise is
a daily occurrence
taken for granted.
Even an "ordinary"
close of day is
beautiful
with nuances of
color.
Its quiet beauty
is like an
ordinary day
in its usual
course with
its tasks.

There come sunsets of
such magnificence
that we watch with
hearts
uplifted. "Oh," we
breathe, "if only it
could last."

We are not yet
designed to
live at apices
of awareness.

The days of our
years
have routine
work, annoyances,
frustrations,
anxieties
lightened by
kindness,
concern,
devotion,
and often
abiding
love.

Our lives have
moments
of maximum
meaning
when we know
depths
not frequently
plumbed.

These are our
magnificent
sunsets.

They lend a
glow

a dream
a hope
to our
"ordinary" days.

We can do
what we must;
endure
what we must
knowing that
every day
has its purpose;
that we shall
be sustained
by exaltation
of evanescent,
but no less,
eternal
beauty.

March 1973

SWEET WERE ITS WATERS

This is good-bye.
You are going to a
never never land
of your dreams.
You seek the Holy Grail.
May God grant your
quest.

Life's chalice
which eased our thirst
o'erflowed, o'erflowed.
Sweet were its waters
that doubt turned
brackish to the taste.

Now it is half empty;
its spring is dead.

SYMPHONY

None of us can entirely miss it;
some of us brokenly hear it.
On its broad theme could soar
now, and forevermore
the sensitive world
cruelly hurled
into apparent abyss.
It sickens for this harmony it seems
destined to miss.

The theme is recurrent
though no deterrent
to provoking variation,
exchange, subtle mutation.
We vibrate to a height
that threatens by its might
to shatter the frail dimension
that is barrier to comprehension.

Something holds us back;
though fierce the yearning, there is lack
of completion
a demolition necessary
of the union
of body and spirit.

That's why we don't always hear it
that symphony full and complete

now stern, now unutterably sweet.
the body too heavy, the tautened nerve
can't unfalteringly serve
our longing to grow
ineluctably to know
to grasp the intangible
to feel the manacle
of eternity, a component part
to glow and beat with its might heart.

So, humbly to listen
praying for vision
that the barrier be broken
the word be spoken.
We sense that symphony never distorted
the clear full melody always supported.

December 1937

174

SYNTHESIS

Black on white or
white on black
is easy to
see. There are
no blurs, nor
indecision
but clear cut
margins and
too obvious
entities.

This view
distorts. It
is incomplete and
illusory.

Red in faint light
is black.
White is all
colors.

With the closest
attention we cannot
determine where
one shade
becomes another.

Let us know that
beneath the exterior
there are forms
superimposed
on each other.

We must not
confuse flatness
with hidden
depth, with
profundity in all
its measure.

With all our effort
imagination
acumen
concepts of
"insideness"
direction
indirection
straight and
undulating
curved and
angular, we
can only approach
the totality of
"isness."

Beyond this
material
inadequate
grasp
is all the
formless existence
of all that
is.

While complexity
is confusing,
there is
comfort
in a
synthesizing
unity.

April 1971

THE AVON—CHRISTCHURCH

The newer Avon is far away
from England's shore
in Island South, New Zealand.
Swiftly flowing
twixt borders neat
it curves
and swings.
Willows in streamers
green, lean
to view, quite pleased
reflections a little blurred
by rounded heads
and bodies sleek
of ducks
that quietly but
swiftly paddle along
oft in erratic course.
Their brown bills
seek morsels sweet.
Mostly, these ducks,
a fair-sized fleet
share their
watery estate in
unruffled calm,
but sometimes
quack with
hoarse intent
although to others

than ducks
there is humor
in their talk.
They waddle
(and their gait is amusing)
onto banks of green.
Big well-meaning
others
court favor
tossing bits of
bread, or
intriguing
oddments.
Watchers are more
numerous.
On warmer days
the gratuitous
larder is quite
complete.
Some look dour and
dreary.
Shorter daylight
winter hours
even ducks
may shiver
but intuitively
know that
"If winter comes,
can Spring
be far behind?"

January 1970

179

THE BRIDE AT DUSK

Now, let me see
if everything is as it should be.
I'll place another sturdy log
and put the kettle on the hob.
This lamp out of sight
scarce dims the hearth's gay light.
The white cloth of lovely stuff
is beauty enough
with that single rose
in inimitable pose.
The limpid crystal
offsets what's wistful
in that delicate ware
that had a share
in Grandma's courting day
and that bold China trader had his way.
Each knife and fork and spoon placed there
with meticulous and loving care
two of this, and that, and something more
the twoness that's oneness—heart's own core.

It is getting late;
the click at the gate;
the open door, the smiling face
glow and warmth in every place.

Here, oh, here is love.

August 1935

THE GREAT MYSTERY

So now we are exploring Mars.
We know something of that bit
of the universe
more than two hundred million
miles away.

There is an inner mystery
in our skulls, and in
the framework, blood
sinews, nerves, and
integument of our bodies.
It well may be that the facts
of the distant planet
may be easier to understand
than the less than microscopic
facets of
our springs of life.

Learned men can devise
most ingenious theories and
design, but
life always eludes
their grasp. Is there something
less than tenuous
that joins the most distant star
and the impalpable essence that
is we?

When we feel most perplexed
and isolated,
we are aware of the earth
beneath our feet;
we take delight in
birdsong and
glory of flowers. The
water and wind talk to us;
the sun warms us, and the
moon makes beautiful
the earth and heaven.

Bones, ancient beyond imagining;
and artifacts of our ancestors
speak of a primordial life
that has shaped us. The light
of stars burned out for us
held them enthralled.

In ages long past
men sought to understand
their world. Early glimmerings
glowed, enlarged, awakened,
and lured men
to continue the search
for that thing
that would somehow
make them complete
and assure oneness of all.

We continue the quest.

August 1976

THE LONELY HEART

It matters not
where it is
the lonely heart
knows
no peace.
Skies may be
blue;
birds may sing
in lusty beauty
fruitlessly.

Lush green
carpets
receptive earth,
but barren patches
protrude.
Pure springs
sparkle
to become
alas
befouled.

Young beauty
poverty beaten
fades
prematurely
joylessly.

Dreams die
agonizing
in disillusion's
congealing
frost.

The lonely heart
feels
because it
is heavy—touched
with sorrow.

July 1947

THE MILES BETWEEN

What are you doing now
miles across the sea
and a continent away?
Your body in a chair or
bed? (for you cannot walk.)
Your spirit is perhaps
with me?

Words dropped in a box
fly to you
sometimes in forty-eight
hours
two sunrises and nights
between.

Words convey so much
and also so little. The tone
the gesture don't meld
with the symbols.

But both, alas,
spoken or written
are not retrieved.
If joy their import
one does not want them back,
but if there is pain
one would wish them
never said nor sent.

June 1970

THE MOCKER

The mocker tonight
in sunset's glow
is as gay a young fellow
as you are like to know.

His song is a medley
for your ears' surprise;
saucy and pert
he's a delight to your eyes.

Clearly now,
"Come here, come here,"
with peremptory tone.
Then, "When do we eat
alone, alone, alone."

"Pshaw, pshaw, pshaw!
Another day is done,
but I stole a new song
to sing, come the sun!"

June 1936

THE STARS GIVE LIGHT

Everything be it great or small
has an innate vital quality
that you can't name, perhaps, at all.
Is it purpose, evolution, even frivolity?

When to Everyman comes his burden,
his effort seems truly debased.
He questions wrathfully the guerdon.

To ease his care, his inner distaste
he flings himself away from man.
In blackest night he stumbles on
seeking solution if he can
to woes that are leviathan.

But, eternally, the stars give light
to those who see though dark the night.

August 1936

THIS REPETITION

Whence comes this
repetition I feel?
The mockingbird's
present varied song
seems not only
a remembrance of
my years in
this place but
as the sounding
in ears of
long, long ages
past.

When first I saw
the mountains
rising in the sky,
they appeared
not strange. Their
jagged, proud, stern
profile strengthened
feeble purpose,
lured to new
effort that had
grown futile.

So with the sea.
Far away
almost motionless

it sustained me in
reverent awe. It
was immensity,
mystery, eternity,
but it contained
and supported being.
In itself it was
nearly all, but
reflected in its mirror
yet other worlds.

Between was an ether
to us insubstantial
that bore to us
intimations of how
it was in other
spheres. Limited
as we are, it can
transmit
our yearnings for
a higher consciousness
which go on and on
forever.

This earth we tread
is our present home.
In its different
mansions of
forest, desert,
fertile field, and

peopled center
we live.
We see with
intentness
other creations—
little things that
fly and crawl
busily doing
their work.
For the breathing
larger lower creatures
we feel a not unworthy
love. They nourish us
in body and in spirit.
Gratefully we accept and
they so richly recompense
us. Look deeply into
the eyes of your dumb
companion, and you
will feel close to
a power that
moves us all.

When with those
dearest to you
you feel drawn
out of yourself
even as you are
most yourself, something
beautiful

engendered long ago,
invisible, immutable
rises again.
The you, the they
are sweetly
bound on a wheel
of remembrance.
You feel
"I have been there.
I have seen this.
I am as I was.
I am as I am.
I am as I shall be."

June 1971

TIME

Time's pictured as young, then old.
Why has someone never told
the tale how he changes in a flash
when pleasure beckons, or markets crash?

In the dentist's chair with stealthy tread
he moves with feet of lead.
He swaggers with the weight of years
and potters, and stupidly peers.

On a sunny day when children play
in fields of pungent hay,
he skips along with nimble step
and when evening comes, says, "Not yet, not yet."

Baby's face is hot with fever;
the loving mother never leaves her.
Long days and nights she has fought
and only Time knows if for naught.

Neck and neck the favorites run;
two seconds more—a wager won.
A sunset of glory—a mere line in a story.
A harsh word of rebuke, and bitterness takes root.

Why has someone never told
How Time is young, and old?

August 1935

192

TO ELSIE IN TRANSITION

Inert you lie. Your pale face
is nobly chiselled.
When you speak, the words are
slurred, and your thoughts are
afar.

In *your* mind your body is in
distant lands
visited long ago.
You are oriented to a
different time and place.

Suddenly you are with me
here and now.
You who have not walked
in years, say,
"I must get up. Now I can walk."

In some subtle way are you
a life ahead?
After years of
patient suffering
and restraint of limbs
are you experiencing
anticipatory joy?

Docilely you take
what I feed you coaxing
"Just one more spoonful,
only one bite more."

You want to sit up, but
in seconds
you are helped back
to the comfort of your bed.

On hearing the sounds of the cooler
you say, "The river is rising."
I question,
"What river?"
"I don't know; it is
in Egypt, I think."
In my sister's welcoming home
you often believe you are in our
own home.
Home?
Where is it?

Life to eighty-two
has been burdened and sorrowful
has often seemed very long.
Life is only as enduring as a
breath—ending in a sigh.

Our coming and our going
are not by our volition.
Whence do we come?
Whither do we go?

Along the way
we know
transcendent moments.
We would live in them
forever—
but not so.
We are again enmeshed
amidst
the usual and the everyday.

Perhaps in the change
now imminent
you are to know
exaltation
forever.

May 1974

TRANSLUCENT HOUSES

We walk about
in our translucent houses
of souls made flesh.
But you know, as do I,
that that facade
returns confusing
reflections.

Back, down, and deep
in the innermost
room
there am I
in my house
and you in your house.
There is a monitor
who counsels
(unwisely, I think)
"Don't go forth. Don't
touch. Don't feel."

Some venture to open
the curtain and
peep through the bars.
Others have no bars.
A few dare to walk out the door
boldly, with key in hand.

confident of
easy ingress
at will.
They run, walk, skip
responding to
a smile
a beckoning hand.

They who go
glow and sing.
Their words, their gestures
their feelings forge
into a vibrant "I."
An "I" that dims
unless it knows
the flux and reflux
with others
who leave
their translucent houses.

TREE AND MAN

High on a mountain there are
no trees. Lower on the slope
a tiny seed finds its way
into a crevice.
A few grains of earth and moisture
are enough to nurture it.
With more favorable conditions
taller trees gradually
make their stand.
When conditions are right,
we find varying species of trees
commingling.
The "happy commingling" is
our human conception of
what is entirely unconscious
for the vegetative kingdom.

We are led to wonder why
man who is conscious
does not become
social to the extent of accepting
the divergencies of
stature, color, and custom
in human development.

The tree disperses its seed through
wind and flying, crawling, and walking
creatures, but
the range is not very great for
an individual tree.
Slowly many species appear
over a wide area.

Man is mobile in his individuality.
If he finds himself in
crowded, noisome, dehumanizing
circumstances,
he can, if conscious of his
power,
find a new habitat.

A tree gives us
shade, fruit, and
flowering beauty.
The human being can
consciously give
shelter, sustenance, and beauty
to his fellows. He can
do more—he can inspire others.
He can bend his mind
to making earth fruitful. He can

explore all the lands
of the earth and
the mysteries of the
universe. He can
discern the beauty and
differences of peoples.
He can strive ultimately
to achieve a communion of
body, mind, and spirit.

He can be as strong as
the strongest tree, as gentle as
the softest whispering of
pliant leaf, as beautiful as
the fairest flower.
Added to his consciousness
will come an innate response
to the unconsciousness
that produces the seed,
moves it to its destined place,
causes it to grow, and,
finally, to fulfil its purpose
of providing man with
shelter, food, and beauty.

December 1982

UP AND AWAY

(On the Caribbean Sea)

Up and away
to the crossroads of any sea.
Let's see Java, Bali, and the rest
and count us rich whate'er the fee.
Blow, blow, ye brave raw winds
hurl the eternal waters
into white-capped, tortured wrothy witches
flinging spray that glitters.
Remember Cuba, the Pearl
and Bluebeard's Tower, ah me!
o'erlooking the blue blue Atlantic
in fairy Charlotte Amalie?
There's Port au Prince
with its dusky lushness
torrential rains tropic luxuriance
haunted by Christophe's grim fortress.
I want to see the Southern Cross
and phosphorescent spray
the batik sunsets, myriad-colored junks
and the flying fishes play.
Hong Kong, Singapore,
Le Havre, Lisbon, Belise,
Venice, Leningrad, Tampico, Yokohama,
and many others, besides these.
I wish it were easy
to up and away
to lie on coral strands in foreign lands
and dream the livelong day.

June 1938

WATER-SWEPT BY THE SEA
(Burnham-on-Sea, England)

When I alone, alone
would be
let me walk on sands
water-swept
by the sea.
Where, bare, my feet
reap comfort
from earth firm-packed
by tumultuous waters
thundering
in approach
mysterious
their debris.
Harsh and ugly secrets
and beauty, too
companionably mingled
exposed to
healing air and light.

So might we bring
from hidden fissures
dark fragments that
obscure our souls' sun.
In the splendor of
new-found sight
the dark, too,
takes on light.

August 1967

WE SEEK COMPLETION

What am I?
Do you know
what *you* are?

We are told
we are not this body
through which we learn,
but we do know
it has these eyes
with which we see
color, form, motion
in manifold nature
and in most mysterious
beings like, yet
strange, to us.

The ears delight us
with lovely sounds
of bird, water, wind,
and wave. And each
being speaks with his
very own voice
unlike any other
in all this
wide world.

This body demands
always
food and warmth.

To satisfy it we
toil.
So intent are we
in subservience
to it that we
don't think
often
of that other
self that
sees not,
does not hear,
itself invisible
without sound
nor motion
that *is* we.

It is variously
called
spirit, soul,
mind,
conscience,
consciousness.

Whatever its
name
it is elusive.

We seek
but rarely find
etherealized

the vision
the sound
the touch
the taste
that we
sense
in wider but
measureless
dimension.

So, restless and
limited
knowing we
are less than we are
we seek
completion
a coalescence in
new recognition.

January 1971

WHEN I THINK OF YOU

When I think of you,
my tears do flow—
yes, even though
love should comfort me.
For you came to me
through chance, they say
but not that way
does heaven come.
Who knows in what
intricate design
your thoughts were mine
with your vision, too, I saw.
Nor is it strange
the questing heart will know
and ineluctably show
its secret treasure.
In the yearning chambers
of the mind and heart
there is a dart
of lambent fire.
But oh! We're earthbound;
though heavenward
we could soar,
we're bound to the shore
of our limitations.
So, when I think of you,
my tears do flow
nor do I know
love to comfort me.

November 1948

WHEN YOU KISS ME

When you kiss me
a joyous beauty
a vibrant sweetness
pervade my being.

Our life breaths mingle;
time stops. My heart
echoes your heart's beat
when you kiss me.

May 1946

WHERE—WHERE?

Where, where is the place for me?
  Am I too rooted, or am I free
  to fashion my life
  in tempest and strife
  in an alien land?
Will my spirit shrink, or stand
  brave and tall
  neither falter nor fall?
How to tell if the spell
  is lasting and real
  or only a lure to seal
  my doom?
Late or soon
  a place narrow and deep
  will hold me in uneasy sleep.

December 1940

WHILE YET THERE IS TIME

Now I am old.
As I older grow
I know how
precious is
each day.

With lessened force
I appreciate more
the strength that
still is mine
to walk toward
the sunset
to see to read
sustaining thoughts
to laugh at the
funny things
we humans
do and say.

Yes, to laugh even
as bombs
fall
and my people
commit such
wrong.
Whence comes
this power that
propels us
to evil?

I suffer
the wrongs
done
within my
country.
I grieve over
what we do to
people
far away.

I seem so helpless;
you seem so helpless
to change
our course.

How remote
we are from
those who
make decisions
that determine
our lives.

Are we more than
digits
to be controlled?
Are even our
thoughts
our own?
Technology
has made
eyes to see

ears to hear
within us.

"They," "the Man,"
"Power"
would mold
us
would rule
us
completely.

Desperate as the
situation is
we must struggle
and just
maybe
we can
avert total
manipulation
mechanization
dehumanization
annihilation.

It will be a
near thing
for we have
insensibly been
invaded
enmeshed
homogenized
bemused.

But a vital core
resists.
It is now
aroused
alerted.
Its potential
is great.

We must struggle
with all our
might.
We must
unite to
become
what we were
meant to be—
noble
in mind
pure in
spirit and
free.

May 1972

WHY DO I LOVE YOU?

Why do I love you?
Darling, for so many things.
You are so good, so true
and then you are you!
There is no eye that is so clear, so dear;
no touch so tender as your own.
Your heart's quick sympathy
is shown in your understanding tone.
Your quick, keen mind
finds an answer
for every kind
of problem.
You are so human.
Yours is no academic mind
that dryly considers
graphs and curves
mediums that serve
to obliterate the significance of
the man, the woman, the child.
The saints of old, gentle, mild
must have been like you
in mind and heart
with GOOD shining through.
I love you for these many things;
all of them are true.
And then, besides, you are you!

November 1946

WIND AND RAIN

Wind and rain still sustain
a duality of function.
Seldom do they separate
and then with odd compunction.
Sometimes rain starts the sally;
more often, wind sets the beat
now fast—now slow
that sends them down the street.
They are frolicsome and full of fun;
let Mr. Importance lose his hat!
Merrily they scurry on
with cognizance of this and that.
Many an anxious eye roves the sky
to wonder about the weather.
Wind scuds dark cloud;
but sun peeks around. So whether—
To take a reefer on the run?
Leaving it is sure to be wrong
for rain coyly lowers her lashes
and big tears course along.
Oftimes their scourge is strenuous
leaving devastation's mark
where floods in mad rush descend
wind rips and tears. It is a lark.
Man, though a crafty creature,
is ever puny in the face
of union of nature's forces.
Who gambles on the race?

December 1936

WINTER WIND

Shielded by familiar
walls
warmed by fire's
heat and glow
I listen to the winter
wind.
It is sad tonight.
It speaks with
throaty, angry voice,
a roar!
Then it rises in
pitch, a keening
sound, razor shrill.
It fingers some
inner nerve
that thrills to
the unknown.
I relive primordial
fears.
My senses are
inordinately
alert.

The air relentlessly
impelled
plucks the
strings of mountain

and valley. Great
trees pulsate in
mighty unison.
The old among them
with sap run thin
snap with
sharp staccato.

Icy cold
the air
ruffled waters
are frozen so.
They become
enormous
washboards
on which the whole
town's laundry could
be rubbed.

Tall stacks of
chimneys
brace for
resistance.
Some lose
the struggle and
broken rubble of
bricks litters the
streets at
dawn.

Old-fashioned lights
on slackened wire
swing in
crazy arcs.

Isolated houses
meet the full
impact. No friendly
barrier protects the
shutters that
bang, the
shingles that
lose their grip.
The whole windward wall
trembles.

I sit by the fire
immersed in
sound and feel
deep vibrations of the
natural world.
The wind rages about me.
I know its force
but it is vacuously
elemental;
whereas, I
am sentient.
But not
enough, not
enough.

May 1971

217

WOMAN-EARTH

Woman-Earth, thou art
fine, clean,
clear visioned
born of the earth and the sky.
Thou art the burst of the storm
the cool of the evening
the flow of the prairie
the long hill's undulation
the surge of the ocean.

Man on thee
knows the violence
of tropic exuberance
of life over abundant
too exultant
the harsh austerity
of polar cold
and night
the thirst of the desert
the salt of the sea.
All, all
man knows
in thee.

Encompass, Woman-Earth,
with thy myriad body
the stubborn, the seeking,
the aching thrust

of man's
javelined desire
to penetrate
the womb of earth's night.

Oh, Force, Magic, Soul
Substance
of time and space
endless and infinite,
let there be new
sons of man
who *are* the light
who have gentle *might*
who *know*, who *feel*, who *see*
they are ONE IN THEE!

January 1944

YEARNING

I seek.

A constant yearning
pushes my eye to greater vision
strains my ear to new vibration
tautens my groping hand.

I'm akin to the bursting seed
the crowding grass
the reaching wind
the ceaseless tide.

Perhaps to become
the fallen fruit
the grass in cere
the quiet calm
the waters stilled.

I yearn.

March 1957

YOU SEE . . . I LOVE YOU

As the sun's warm rays
effect my delight
so does your glowing
heart
infuse a nascent joy,
impart a new-found
radiance.

The wind's soft pinions
bring fragrance,
but no sweeter
than emanations
from the tender
flowers
nurtured in the
secret garden of your
soul.

Music? It is
your voice
finding its swift unerring
way
to my wakened
heart.

You see, I love you.

February 1945

YOUTH TO YOUTH

Do you love me?
Answer true.
I pray to God
you do.
I never meant to
tell you now
but how
with those eyes
of dew
can any man help
asking you?

I'm poor, you know,
and that's a blow
to your Dad.
It won't make your
Mother glad.
I'm poor, you know,
though I adore you so—
your Mother and Dad—
what will they say
when I take you away?

But my heart knows joy;
my pulse is young
with all my soul it sings
come—come!